Finding Home

Cecilia Knapp

This edition published by BX3 an imprint of
Burning Eye Books 2017

www.burningeye.co.uk
@burningeyebooks

Burning Eye Books
15 West Hill, Portishead, BS20 6LG

ISBN 978-1-911570-17-2

Cecilia Knapp is a writer, poet, performer and educator. She's performed her work all over the UK and internationally and at festivals such as the Edinburgh Fringe, Bestival and Camp Bestival and the Cheltenham Literature festival, where she was guest curator in 2016. She's had a residency at the Roundhouse, had her work played on BBC radio 1, 1Xtra and radio 4 as well as being commissioned by the TATE and BBCiplayer. Cecilia writes about real life, every day human interaction, experience and relationships. She tackles loss, love, bereavement and mental illness in her work, believing in the power of sharing stories and how they can heal and unite us. She is an ambassador for the mental health charity C.A.L.M.

Aliet Hilary —
with Love
x
thanks —

Cecilia
xxx

Finding Home was first brought to life on stage in October 2015 at the Roundhouse, with the following creative team:
Performer: Cecilia Knapp
Director/Dramaturgy: Stef O'Driscoll (Nabokov, A Tale From A Bedsit, Kate Tempest's Hopelessly Devoted)
Original Music: Bellatrix and Peter Knapp
Musical director: Chris Redmond (Tongue Fu)
Visual Design: Charlie Carr-Gomm

The visuals in this edition of Finding Home are by Charlie Carr-Gomm

As always, for Leo. Forever Love.

I am part of all that I have met
-Tennyson, Ulysses

PART ONE

It's raining. Well, drizzling. And a thin film
of moisture clings to my skin. I'm cycling.
And my dad's words start ringing in my ears
in his thick bass baritone.
You know you really should wear a helmet. And get your gears fixed.
My dad is the kind of man who doesn't trust a dishwasher.
Too much of a helping hand, he says.
I'm soaking wet now. But the canal
is beautiful & calming; and I need this.
The trees reflect on the water and it's almost as though they're
breathing. My heart swells again with a love for London that I
knew was hiding somewhere
under my ribs.
So I keep on.

Hot car seats. Faint smell of dog. Time stretching out like chewing
gum. M1. Cassette tape on.
It's Patsy Kline. Mum moves the words around her mouth
and taps her index finger on the gearstick
in perfect time.
I'm crazy. Crazy for feeling so lonely ...

I ask her, *why are all the best songs about love?* Her lips curl.
You'll find out one day, she says. And her eyes
dart up to the rear view mirror to check on me
in the back of the car.

I used to love to drive with her.
Wine gums in the glove compartment, poems on tape.
Dylan Thomas was her favourite. Mine's the same.

We'd go to her parents on the border of Wales
and swim in lakes. I would smoke cigarettes
in the tree-house with the girls next door and we would rub our
fingers on rosemary bushes to mask the smell.
As if that was any use.

My big brother Hal would look at me through his curtain fringe; knowingly. I only saw him a few times a year.

All the eagerness to impress that our age gap brings would force me to avoid eye contact and pretend I like Oasis. My dad still talks of those times even now. Playing Elgar on car journeys, he'll never exceed 70 miles an hour. Six week summers now seem like a double exposed film. Shoulders become heavier as years press themselves against you.

I've only ever seen him cry once.

Now it annoys me how long it takes him to roll a cigarette. He smokes it right down to the end until the cardboard roach begins to burn, whilst mine lays bent double in the ashtray still breathing slightly.

I only smoke when I'm with you he says, wrinkled fingers reaching into yellow packet, a long scar
down one thumb; an allotment war wound.

And when I was with your Mother, there was always a packet of 10 Marlborough under the tea towels in the kitchen drawer.

When we were kids, he sang through all the hard times. His voice filled Sundays. Sailed over unpaid bills and tantrums over hand-me-downs.

Days that throbbed with music. He breathed it. Car boot full of manuscripts. Sellotaped glasses. Pencils. Pianos. Pockets. He'd tell me stories of the operas. The love and the pain.

These are real stories. This is real life, he'd say.

I always knew I wanted to write stories. That I would do that one day. That when I wrote stories, I somehow felt ok. When I was older, I used to ask him *why can't you just be a postman? At least then we'd make our rent. Wouldn't have to worry about the TV being taken away by bald men with massive shoulders.*

He is whiskers & twinkling. There is youth behind his creases. He'll feel for a lighter that doesn't exist in the depths of his pockets and I will sigh and pass my clipper across the pub bench towards him.

One pint Spitfire. Two pints Spitfire. Half pint Guest ale. Whisky. That's his lot. It's always been the same. We used to tease him for it.

I'm back on the canal now in the rain and I can barely see the
path in front of me. The sky continues to fall on me. Lights in the
distance spread themselves into my squinted eyes and make stars
of streetlights.

Last night, the tips of Hackney spires were beginning to tickle the
pink skyline. The bus sighed. I sat next to a man I thought I could
maybe love. He pushed my hair to the side. I thought of all the
things I was trying to hide from him. And of the love I was trying
to find. His heart seemed open at first, so mine soon followed
suit. Unlocked the little gate around itself and leapt out, palms
outstretched. Desperate to be held.

He looked out at the steamed up, rain speckled wind screen on the
top deck of the bus, profile on, no eye contact, muscles moving in
his jaw.
Yeah ... I can't do this anymore, he said. So I just feigned nonchalance
and rang the bell; stepped out into the night and let the sinking
feeling melt me down like sticky paint for double yellow lines.
City tarmac. Something else gone. And London is a photo album
of kisses on corners and memories. It won't let me move on.

Meg's always asking me about the state of my heart.
She's been like a sister since Year 7 science class.
Mr Turner. Melting pens with Bunsen burners.

When I was growing up in Brighton with her, Ladies night was
my girls and Fridays. Pink wine bought by my dad. Blue plastic
bag and a 10 deck of fags. Catching last sunlight through pastel
terraces, all crowded into a bedroom too small for us, drinking
wine from mugs, mattresses laid down on the floor waiting for our
return from sticky bars and cold chips at 4 am. We'd talk. Fifteen
year-old girls on a Brighton terrace at the mouth of the world,
just staring in. Dancing under strings of sea-front lights drinking
capfuls of gin, thinking we knew what's to come.

Far from the chaos of fifteen, she often sat at the bar in front of me
as I polished glasses.

Top up? I ask.
How are you doing?
Yeah I'm doing ok.
How are you really?

It's funny what we tell ourselves to get by. All these little lies, these platitudes, like worn out carpet. *Tomorrow is another day.* Or, *good things come to those who wait.* But what if it feels like all your tomorrows are turning into yesterdays? Love to me so far has been the aching of a loss. All the buses that never stopped. And the ones I forgot to get off.

Walking home through discarded jumpers
and cigarette butts, with a stitch in my gut and acid reflux, I think of lost loves. How when I go to take the plunge, my heart stops - but with all the banality of looking down for a watch when you've forgotten to put it on. How long am I going to be waiting for? Because I still see certain faces in the loneliness of late night train stations. The kinds of places where there's just a bench. An ancient poster. And something quiet will pour from me in the dark. Like they're reaching out their arms. The kind of stillness we all long for everyday.

It's Friday. And I push on in the rain to the pub. I'm 10 minutes late but I slip through the back and the bosses are already drunk. The air weighs a ton.
As I approach my side of the bar, Dave rests a heavily ringed finger on the beer mat. He sinks the rest of his ale and raps on the bar - ring sovereign side down - for another. Drunk now and on to how the East End isn't how it used to be. The Jews have gone and it's all Muslim graffiti on his shutters every couple of weeks. His beard is sticky with bitter now and he's on to yet another. On to the gays. How he knew one who worked at a pub down the road who had AIDS.

And these days they're even more shameless, he says.
These days they're getting married; like they're the same as us.

He scrapes the hate from the back of his throat. And she stands proud beside him. Nodding and wincing with each sip of sparkling wine. Her make-up - over the course of a day spent in conversation with the deep fat fryer - has fallen into the crow's-feet around her eyes. She nods to his sermon. They've been married 25 years. But from what I overhear, in-between drinks and thick elbows propping up the bar, they seem only to discuss what they fear. I don't know. I guess not all love is the same. There are different types. Different names.

J was the first person I loved completely in the way that makes
you feel a bit sick. The way that makes you lose your integrity
and get a bit pathetic. I wonder if I'll ever feel the same as I once
did on Sunday mornings with him. Sharing cigarettes and cups
of tea with ashtrays on naked stomach skin. Fickle city light on
windowsills. Boxer shorts. Thighs wrapped around shins. And
immediately, I think of all the places where I have held someone.
Hackney silhouettes. Kensal Rise. The starlings over the sea.
I remember the shapes of their shoulder blades.
I hope that they remember me.

I've polished a glass so hard, I notice a spot of blood beginning
to emerge from my knuckle. It's fanning out like a spider's web
in lines across my fingers. I put the glass down. A little too hard.
Swallow. Take a credit card. Crunch a Pork Scratching beneath my
toe. Turn to go to the back room.
Between naked cardboard ladies with peanuts hanging off them,
I breathe. Sit on an upturned bucket next to stacks of compilation
driving-rock Cds.
I think of my brother Leo. And his stories of stolen nights in salty
air, hating being different.
A gay man in Brighton still can't feel safe. Getting in to strangers
cars under cover of night.

Better that way than to admit it.

Cruising Brighton seafront for situations that would hurt him.
Holding older men in the darkness of pub alleys. His deep-set
hazel eyes that struggled to consume the world. To let it make
sense to him. Those who hate the Different stand behind this door.
Their *'faggots!'* thrown so carelessly from their tongues.

I wouldn't be happy if it were my son.
All I'm saying is, they can do what they like so long as I don't have to
watch.

These voices fill my weekly pay packet. They stand there.
Drinking-in humid beers and nodding their heads at breezeblock
headlines; words strong enough to create cracks in sky-high
buildings and leave the sediment to settle in hearts. London rent
forcing me to compromise. I am now a dab-hand at changing
barrels and holding my tongue.

An empty chair at my Christmas table.

Hours pass. I look out at the bar. Punters crunched over their pints
like used-up greaseproof paper. Iron filings to a magnet. Old Jack
in the corner. His face a script. A scarecrow stuffed with Rizlas and
old betting slips. Sips his half pint as the bottles clink in bags for
life around his feet. Tobacco under fingernails.
I wonder if Leo had stuck around, whether this is what he'd be
doing now?

Dad. Teaching us to cycle down a hill, unaided.
He'd let me go first, slipping away the scarf he was using to
guide me and all I could do was pedal, try to keep straight. White
knuckles gripping handle bars, looking to the end of the road, just
trying to keep going. We used to smoke out of the windows
in Dad's Mondeo, shouting at cyclists. Dad says
change is the only thing you can rely on.

I reckon he's on to something there.

Tinned fruit. Chinese burns. Sun-sore skin, compasses, gut
punches. Pebbles. How far can you pull the skin down around
your nails? Until it bleeds? *Grandmothers' blessings* we used to call
them.

I wash a final glass. Blistered feet and a heavy heart. Leave after
midnight. It's still raining thick & fast.
I watch the bus driver finish his night shift. Switch off the light in
the cabin, and sit. The city silent like a crypt.

I look up, lick the rain water from my lips. Cycle past Hackney
Wick. This is existing in the madness of it.

PART TWO

Bedtime stories.

Me and Leo under Lion King covers.

I get my nail under the plastic of one of those glow-in-the-dark stars that clings to the wall. I test it to try and prise it free without pulling plaster. I know it will make a mark if I keep on pulling, but still I do.

Leo's eyes widen. Pools that throw back to me the glare from the landing.

I'm gunna tell on you.

I convince him not to by holding a crucial piece of scalextric hostage. We make up new branches of our Toytown dramas. Big Ted and Little Bear are in a loveless marriage.

Maybe he has an affair?

I learned this term while watching ER, in secret, from the stairs. Later, it'd be a bit closer to home and we'd split our weekends between the Midlands and the South coast. Dad will explain to me one day over a third cup of lukewarm Earl grey. He will try to tell me why.

I will be old enough to look him in the eye and tell him he taught me the greatest lesson in life.

He is human. So am I.

The black cat from the Beanie baby family has run away. Me and Leo decide to run with that storyline this week. Last week Reco the dog was given the role of secret agent in an attempt to thwart the evils of the new kitten. Tinkle. Leo had her in one hand and the potato masher in the other, until mum intervened.

It's 1998. And this is my entire world.

Ten years later the bed we lie on is in a different city. The sheets are peeling off. Smoke curls from our mouth and chicken boxes scream our state out. The bones tell on us as we roll roaches. He wants to get clean. *Start exercising*, he tells me. Finally get a couple of GCSEs. Beanie pulled low. Deep eyes and ripped jeans and a mouth the same shape as mine. I see glimmers of *The Lion King* days flash over his face.

When I need to talk to him, I go to the kitchen. Dad keeps his
tobacco on top of the fridge. He buys the soft stuff from the fancy
tobacconist. Pretends it's not communal, but it is. Leo and I roll it
between our fingers and stand side-by-side leaning over the stable
door. We live so close to the shore we can smell the sea when we
light up.
What are you afraid of?

When we were growing up, other boys in the cul-de-sac found
each other in the universality of kicking ball. They'd compare
bleeding knuckles and their dads' porn. Saved up for dirt bikes
to ride by the Marina and made up stories of blow jobs. He made
friends with those who existed on the outskirts. Rode buses to
squats.

Leo's a disruptive presence in the classroom Mr Knapp.
We have tried several methods of behaviour management.
Mr Knapp, Leo's not been getting along with his peers very well.
Is everything alright at home?
*I'm afraid we don't really have much choice at this point, we just don't
have the resource.*

You didn't go again?
No.
What did you do all day?
Dunno.
Do you want some dinner?
No.
Leo?

He spent days in places
where the height of tower blocks
towered over aspirations.
Older men stationed in stairwells.
Blue tattoos on their hands,
they showed emotion with their fists.
Apathy. Split lips.

I told him about my first kiss.
The first boy I'd been with.

He feigned a shocked face.
Asked for all the details.
Crossed his legs,
sat bolt upright
and adopted the character of a
simpering sex education teacher.

Now Cecilia. It's perfectly normal for you to have these urges.

Pillow chuck to his head.
He used to pick out my clothes for me.
You look lovely in green.

On Saturdays I would sit in his room,
recounting my dreams.
He'd nod and roll weed
in a piece of cereal packet
shaped like an M.
He smelt of cigarettes and damp towels.

Dad's made risotto again.

Fuck's sake. He always does that.

Are you ok?

Yeah. I guess.

What's going on, in your head?

I don't know.

And have you thought any more, about seeing someone?
Someone, I don't know, to help you make sense of it all?

I don't need to see anyone.

Please don't hurt yourself again. Just promise me that.

Don't be stupid.

Just say it.

You need to hear me say it?

Say you won't do it again.

I won't do it again.

I love you, you muppet.

I love you too.

Shall we get KFC?

Yeah, I'll come with you.

Friends came and went. Volatile relationships mainly. Sarah was the only one who stuck around. She knocked on our door one summertime. Her circumstances weighing heavy on her. The way heavy boots affect the way you walk. She'd come to use our shower. Borough street Brighton. Number 7. Paint eroded from salt air, scruffy shrubs in the front garden.

She was getting changed with the door unlocked, when I walked in. But she didn't cover her body. Didn't seem to possess the ability to be embarrassed. They were best friends from then on in. I don't know where he found her. She was tolerant. She liked ketamine. That pretty much fitted the bill for him. She was missing a tooth at the front of her mouth. But her face was kind and open and smooth and loving; like she had so much to give. It was just, that in her life so far, no one had wanted to take any of it. She'd had a baby a couple of years before. *Not fit for motherhood* they'd said. She was on the mend though, she had to be. But each weekend would roll itself under them and knock them off their feet, and I'd find them curled-up in the front room, resisting sleep with videogame home screens on repeat.

She said she found home in number 7 Borough Street. In all its grubbiness. And I did too. We had a futon and a lawn chair in our front room. *Throw a blanket on it, no one will know the difference* Dad said as it creaked underneath him. Incense burning.

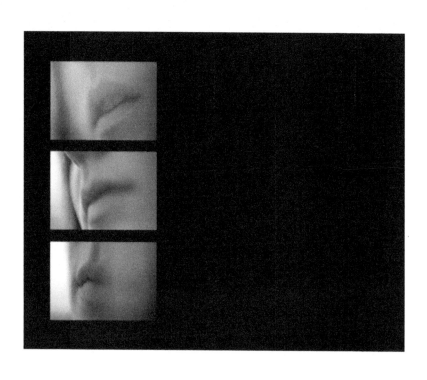

I often wonder how many feet of the Displaced crossed our
doormat. Leo brought them in. Shared spliffs with them and
listened to their stories. Shared his with them. Made them feel like
they were worth the time. Fervent voices on futons with curtains
drawn. Cross-legged on rugs. Ashtrays made from empty packets.

Once, when we'd both lost our keys, he found a homeless guy to
break-in. I'd chased Leo out of the house on a quest for rizla.
You've got your keys right?
No dickhead. You?
You're joking. What the fuck are we going to do?
He stood there in his dressing gown, no shoes. Laughing as
whisky breath billows into salt air and the more I panic, the more
he doesn't care. Suddenly he's off round the corner on to Western
road, trackies hanging low, cords of his dressing gown whipping
the night like some crazed bedroom superhero.

RIZLAS FIRST, YEAH? He yells over his shoulder and darts into
the Turkish shop. He comes out grinning; I can tell he's drunk.
'Scuse me mate, can you do us a favour? He's leaning into a guy
sitting on the steps of Norfolk square.
We just need someone to just climb up through my bedroom window.

I hiss Leo's name.
You're fucking serious? I say.
The guy creaks to his feet.
Next thing I know he's walking up our street.
Leo's got his arm around his shoulder and before I know it,
I see the soles of his feet disappearing through the open window,
then I'm grappling with a tense thirty seconds before I hear the
lock click on our front door and the face of the stranger, smiling,
welcoming us into our home.

He stayed all night and told us stories of each tattoo on his arm.
We fed him mugs of some anonymous alcohol we found in a
cupboard and nodded with each inhale / exhale of cigarette as he
told us how he had a daughter but he can never see her. When the
sun came and brought condensation to the windows, we gave him
a loaf of bread from the freezer, a pre-rolled spliff and a fiver.
We never saw him again.

I suppose with the sepia of nostalgia,
the distance that hindsight brings,
this now seems exciting.
But I left this life for London.
That wraps itself around me.

I'm back on the cycle path. I push my pedals down in constant
rhythm and think of when my rent is due. Grip on tighter to the
handles of mum's bike; I inherited it last June. I wonder if my
mum had ridden these streets too? This bit by the canal that joins
Hackney with Tower Hamlets. She rode this same bike in her
twenties. With each turn of the pedal, I feel closer to the answers I
will never get to ask her.
I spent my teenage years seeking mother figures in women on
the bus. Imagining what it would be like to have one? Charlie's
mum sewed a button back on my jeans the other day. *I can't believe
no one's ever taught you how to do this* she said. *You have to wind the
extra thread around the stitch to make it strong.* I looked at her hands
working away, the hands of a mother, weathered from the years.
And tough.

I read somewhere that *'gone'* is the saddest word in the English
language.

It gets easier. You just get little reminders sometimes. Gunfire to
the heart in Tesco Metro when I smelt her old perfume by a tray of
carrots. It's the tiny things. No one really ever told us what to do
without her, you know.

My mother's hands were the same as mine.
When I inherited the bike,
I found typewritten poems in a box of her things.
She used to write too.
When I first tried to put in to words how I felt, I wrote it down on
scraps of paper and read it out.
When I heard it out loud I found
that it didn't matter quite so much anymore.

So I moved. To rooms with wallpaper ceilings bloated from damp and parties in cold flats and carparks. Six of us in the back of a black cab, two crouching on the floor to save money. White lines on DVD cases. Warm rum and ginger in plastic cups. Levi 501s. In love. Out of love. 19. Lips that taste like metal over concrete kisses on the balconies of overpriced privately owned tenement blocks. Lingering hands on the central line. Miriam's had three glasses of wine and she's ready for a fight.

This man just tried to touch my vagina! She shouts to the crowded tube carriage. The culprit looks away. Ducks under an arm at Bethnal Green and slips off into the hot air of the tube station. In the carriage there's a mixture of stifled laughs from freshers, concerned faces and oblivious commuters plugged-in, wired-up and desperate for home. I laugh, take her hand and pull her off at Mile End.
Well if you don't make an example of them, who will? It was the same when we lived in Whitechapel. I mean, Fuck Off!
She tells me she needs a piss and squats down in the street.

I've known her since we were seven. From when I moved to Brighton to live with Dad. She gave me a hard time to prove I wasn't a sympathy case. We shaved our eyebrows off, attempting a sophisticated shape. Sang the Fugues to each other, recorded it on computers and listened back, learning how to harmonise. We turned our bedrooms into shops. We watched a girl give a boy a blow job in the park when we were walking her dog. We rented VHSs from Video Box on Station hill; the dodgy guy working there let us rent 18s; we stuffed weed into the ends of cigarettes that older boys had bought us and thought we knew what it was like to be actually high, she stroked my head when the boy I thought I loved started going out with an older girl in Year 9 and I couldn't afford the Converse I thought would make him love me; I used to carve his name and mine into science benches with a compass; he had hair like Kurt Cobain.

We stuck fake nails on and wore blue eyeliner. Made up boyfriends. Mine, a Johnny Depp type, my buzzwords being *'thoughtful'* and *'glasses'*, hers, was a hench guy with a shaved head. We shared beds. I sucked my thumb. She had a scarf that she threaded between her toes to help her sleep.
We both still do that now.

Slightly later, as fifteen year-olds in Brighton, it was half a pill
and a grope on the Waltzers on Brighton pier. Warm beer, black
roots and peroxide hair. Still very questionable eyebrows (they
took ages to grow back properly) and always, the feeling that our
experience was distinct. We thought we knew it all.

Eyebrows. Cold Chips. Gin. Brixton.

We always said we'd live together.
When we were at school drinking coffees
and pretending they weren't bitter....

We left Brighton together. She couldn't wait
to get started on life. I said the same
but I guess in hindsight, I was running away.
She went to Brixton, me to Lewisham.
The P4 bus ran all night between our doors.
As we rode up the hill
from Dulwich to Brixton one day,
the sun filled up that little single decker,
I grabbed her arm and leaned into her. *We made it.*
We spent days doing what we thought we should do
to live a London life. Nights chasing drugs wrapped in lottery
tickets and new rooftop bars in Peckham

This place smells like actual piss Miri.
And I just paid five pounds for a can of Carlsberg. CARLSBERG!
Yeah well Tom said it was good, and that everyone was coming so…
Oh well if Tom said it was good then it must be good…
what the fuck are we doing here?

We'd spend Saturday mornings with
mouths tasting of onion and sore heads soothed with cans of coke
and anecdotes from night bus rides.
I had this little flat above a hairdressers.
We'd talk about falling in love queues at chicken shops.

I think we both knew it was a one night stand we mutually acknowledged
it.
He didn't hug me, he just gave me a nod.
Said he had to leave for a football match.
Well thank God.
He was rank.

Her cackle carried itself through the skylight and rang around the alley off Lewisham high street. Later we found a place in Whitechapel. Two-hundred quid a month for a flat that smelt of burnt oil and had cockroach shells on the tops of the cabinets. We sugar soaped the walls for three days and lit cheap scented candles which we bought from the corner shop with three bottles of red wine - so shit it looked like Ribena.

Two years of London living. Half-way to a degree.
I was serving overpriced cocktails to a Dalston crowd when the phone call came. I'd had different jobs. Catering and pop-up bars. I couldn't hear my phone vibrate over *Tribe Called Quest* filling up the room from shabby sticky lino to ironic lampshade. Fingers were stinging from crushing lime into plastic cups and filling them with fistfuls of ice for mojitos. It wasn't until I went to the stock room for cans of ginger beer that I glanced at my phone; countless missed calls from a number I didn't know

Hi ... it's Harry from up the road.
Yeah, I don't know how to say this.
You need to come home. Back to Brighton.
He's done it ... You know.
It's Leo.

Gut punch.
I didn't go back enough.
I fell in love in London.
I worked.
And spent nights watching light creep through cheap curtains.
Sticky coffee tables.
Wrapped up.
I was distracted.

After it happened, the days were hollow like the sound of a drum in church. Like we were living in the reverb. Forming scar tissue whilst the world carried on without us. We sat down a lot. Sat down in silence. Extenuating circumstances and compassionate leave. I could have done that for weeks - resisting the call to go back to normal.
Resisting dignity. Trying to stretch out an allocated window of grief that is silently imposed by society. Not wanting to have to function properly. Wanting it to be ok to do strange things like sleep all day and do nothing but eat freeze-dried noodles and drink tea.

People passed through the house. The countertops a constant bed for rings of spilt tea and stacks of teabags.

Time felt heavy. Fell on us like fat raindrops. Splashed on our skin, cold. We drank whiskey in the evenings by the stable door where I used to smoke with him. Faces like empty restaurants. It helped us sleep. It helped us talk. Made the corners blurry, eyelids heavy.

Then that two seconds in the morning when you forget what has happened before you've woken up properly.

The presence of death turned us into a pack. We sat and fed together on easy meals and lapped tea. Arms around me, like I needed to be held together by the weight of something; men turned into alpha males, all logistics, no weeping. Car parking. Hiring things. Legal. Women turned into walking scrap books. Aunties pouring memories and what ifs out of themselves like they were broken taps.

I sat somewhere in between the weeping and the planning. And in a way I enjoyed it. Those few days where it was all about the pain. All about him. We didn't have to do normal things. I could sit and talk about him until my throat gave way. I could shout and weep and bang the wall with my fists and it would be acceptable. I can't do that now.

Neighbours and family would all talk through the night. Try to find some reason. People would throw their contributions around the room:
Some people are only meant to survive for a short while.
He was unhappy.
He was always a difficult child.
Never the same as the other boys.

Passers-by were awkward. We got used to deflecting questions about saving him, brushing them off like thank you for coming, yeah, nodding, yeah, we're coping; yeah it's a beautiful street we've been here years; yeah, you can see the sea; yeah and it's near Waitrose; thank you I'll put them in water - trim the ends yeah, they'll last longer; and have you eaten? And thank you. And thank you for being here. And yes it hurts but we'll be fine.

And then the night.
Could I have saved him?
No the first thing they tell you is not to ask yourself that.
But could I have saved him though?
And could we have done something?
And you tried.
And yeah, yeah I tried but did I try hard enough?
Did I push far enough?
God, you tried your best.
But how do I know?
How do I know if that was good enough?
And will I ask myself this forever?
And I ask myself this for what feels like forever in quiet moments.
Twelve young men every day did you know that?
1 in 4, did you know the stats?
In the UK?
Yeah, right here. It's happening every day and we are blind to it.
Shit.
And it's better this way.
Perhaps it's better this way.
Maybe we would be the selfish ones for wanting him to stay?
No it's brave, isn't it brave?
Or it's the cowards way out.
Yeah could you do it though?
Could you really do it?
Can you ever imagine feeling that low?

A Saturday. The house full of people acting as distractions.
Replacing wilting flowers. A chilli on the stove. Shouting for
parking permits. And can we do anything? And it's fine, we're all
fine, we're making arrangements.

When my skull couldn't contain it all, I would escape to the sea.
Looking out at the expanse of water has a way of making you
feel tiny. Like there's bigger stuff out there. But the smell of the
sea brought a sickness. A stone in my stomach. How can this
place exist without him, sat on hot tarmac with him in Brighton
summertimes? Twos on a rollie, silver rizlas made them see-
through and his eyes were amber in the sunsets.

I watched the birds dart through the bones of the burnt-down pier. I watched children run to the shore and retreat, screaming as the waves went for their toes. I inhaled the wet, flat expanse of sand, slight smell of tar, salt and fish. Pebbles. I heard the crunch of shoes on beach behind me and stiffened with the anticipation of company.

Couldn't quite work out whether I wanted it. It was J. The familiarity of the shape of his teeth, the smell of him, filling up my body.
J searched me with his eyes. Darker brown than Leo's and always wide. You know, I still wear J's jumpers. Even now.

I met him dancing in a bar with the walls painted black. And in my head I am still there sometimes. December cold that dulled my ear lobes. The sanctuary of steamed-up windows. We sat shoulders touching in the garden. The smell of damp coats and beer and rum & coke. He traced his fingers over the tattoo on my wrist and that was the first time I let him in. I told him Mary Anne was my mum. That we'd lost her years ago. Later, I would tell him everything.
I picked up a handful of pebbles, blind. If I open my hand and it's an even number, I'll be fine.

Seven pebbles.
Try again.
Nine.

You can't keep looking for people to save you whilst pretending you're alright.
J looks at me with brown eyes. Tongue rests on his top tooth. Always does after he's said something loaded. Like he's trying to prove he can handle what he's saying. Still, I'm not sure if he'll ever really understand this. If anyone ever will. If even I can.

Before. Lying chest to chest with him. Lewisham. Warm skin. Hearts beating at their own rhythm but somehow still in synch. I used to read him poems from this anthology. That line always stuck with me.
I'll love you till the ocean is folded and hung up to dry.

The other night was one of those nights where you take it all too far. My mate George and I lay on my bed. Clenched jaws. We'd danced until our feet were sore; I had blisters on my soles. We'd crawled home talking shit about how to love when you're so young and all the mistakes other people had made. Light was beginning to pour through the window; the curtains couldn't contain it. Dust rising up in the light lines and settling back down between floorboard cracks. He asked me if I'd ever been in love?

Once.
You?
Never. I don't know if I can do it. Like I don't have it in me.
Do you think that anyone can really understand us, underneath it all?
Sometimes I don't think anyone ever will. It's like I'm scared to give too much of my heart away. Like what if there's not that much left to give?

My asking was a kind of pleading. He nodded. Reached out and placed a hand on my forehead.

My eldest brother and I. Siblings left behind. We sat next to each other at the funeral. The eulogy implored everyone to love each other more. To tell each other that. How you don't know which days will be your last. We shifted in our pews. Stifled coughs. Knowing we don't say these things to each other enough. Life gets in the way. P45s and motorways. I should tell him how I feel. But the truth is, I'm scared of what he'll say.

Black bathwater, muddy from his rugby shins.
Sharing tinned peaches for pudding with him.
Gut punches. Chinese burns.

He is eight years older than me. We have the same ears. When I was a baby, he used to scoop me out of the bath in a towel and pretend I was a sausage roll.

It's harder for boys to lose someone, apparently. Because boys aren't supposed to cry. *Boys don't cry. Grow some balls. Man up.* Clenched jaws that are red with the effort of withholding emotion. Teeth ground down. Clenched jaws. Clenched fists. Clenched heart. This would be the perfect place to start if it wasn't so hard. He stares to the front of the chapel. Why is it so hard to say how we feel?

I wanted to watch lines in Leo's face start with a suggestion then entrench themselves in the places where you smile. Then to see his hair start to grey around the ears. Silver stars in jet black. A breathing paradox. Telling me to give up smoking with a fag in his hand, the centre of attention in any room. Losing him was like the feeling of finishing the last page of an all-consuming book. I'd been reading him for the longest time. It consumed me. Filled my mind. Turning the page to find the last page blank took my breath away.

The worst thing I think about losing someone is the fear that you'll forget them. Because you don't keep scrap books of anecdotes or even photos predicting the knowledge they'll be gone before you've had a chance to exhale. To prepare. You don't have time to remember everything and you can't. And sometimes it's only the dark things you remember, the bruised things, the time he pushed you down the stairs, or claimed he didn't love you, or drank himself into a corner and waded into the sea.

Your mind will try to override the times you rubbed his shoulders for hours because he felt so sad, or the times you invented worlds and stories and restaurants for stuffed toys or 90s house tunes and bike rides. Dressing up in clothes we bought from charity shops, pretending we were ancient gods, the songs we made up on road trips that we humoured dad with. The time I bit his thumb fighting for a pog. And hot milk and honey; spaghetti hoops and Lion King.

The time he came out and he was happy about it for once and we pretended he'd have a boyfriend and we'd all do lunch. And car journeys and cassette tapes and sleeping top-to-toe and crying about Titanic and playing Mario. Drinking red wine on Borough street. And you hear weird things about memory. How you're just remembering the memory and not what actually happened. How you can't choose what you remember. How memories are made in the present moments, how memory is a habit, memory is a conceit. And I can't stand that thought. That I am making up our moments. Our bangers & mash. That I am writing you instead of living you, Leo. That I can't remember everything because it's impossible to. That you're not immediate to me. I want to live with you again so I don't have to look back. So it's right here with me. I wish that you were here with me. I just wish that you were here.
I just wish that you were.
With me.

I can't package this up nicely. I know for me, the only thing that blunts the edge is writing about it. I have to do this.

People are fragile. Some people do not have iron rods to hold them up. And sometimes the world makes you think that there's just so much shit and people are breaking and people are splintering and we're just having to watch it.

And then I feel you with me
and only the good bits. Or,
I meet people who hold me together,
they glue me, they share their bruises with me,
show me their purple and their blues.

And they are hills
and oceans miles deep.
And it is cold tea and sleep.
And they are old CDs and nosebleeds, grazes and nighttime,
drizzle and beats.

Everything. Enormous.
I feel like when it comes to you,
words fail me.
So I just carry you with me.

I get back on the bike. Everything will be alright. For now, sleep. Feet on pedals. Carry on. It's all about carrying on. Look at the moon over the tip of canary wharf. Steam billowing from air con extractors.

Disappearing in to the orange brown sky.

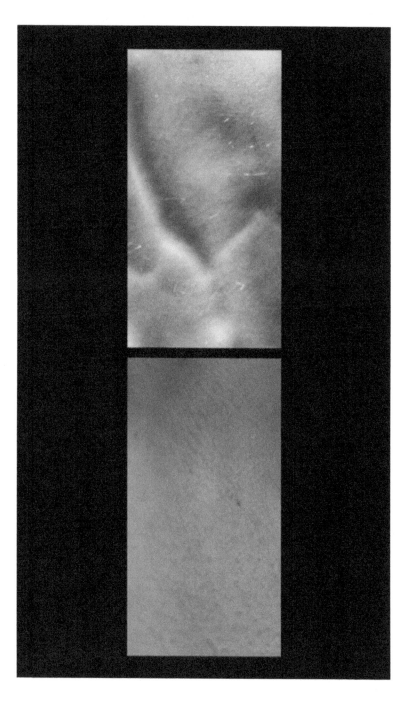

PART THREE

I keep having these dreams. Where I actually say what I feel.
And it always makes everything better.

Back at the pub today, I'm the only person working.
I try to busy myself by sorting
different lengths
of dartboard chalk but there's one punter who wants to talk.
He takes a sip of his Guinness.
The foam sticks in his beard. Without wiping it away,
he looks at me. And lets me know.

You need to smile more babe.

I tell him I don't feel like smiling today.
He replies that I'm starting to get lines on my face.
Tomorrow I might feel like smiling. That's how I carry on. It's hope I guess.
He looks confused. He is holding 20s in his fists like
knuckledusters. Like a punter at a strip club.
Hope. The happiest word in the English language.
Pebbles. Tinned fruits. Black bathwater. Chalk. Scars. Silver Stars.

Someone with a hood up walks past the frosted window. My
heart leaps then sinks again. I will forever see ghosts through
windows. In wing mirrors. In my peripheral vision. In the faces
of newsreaders. And always when I close my eyes with my head
to the pillow. Heart pounding, heavy footfalls on a landing. And
whenever there are sirens outside Mile End station, fire engines,
the grates pulled over the entrance like yellow teeth baring the
way; people complain, late to get to the jobs that they hate. Maybe
they've just left the ones they love, a kiss over cornflakes. I just
hope whoever jumped that day was loved in that way too. I'm
getting used to seeing ghosts. Nowadays it just means I know he's
with me always.

I don't escape to the sea so much these days.
But when I do go down
and sleep with seagulls sounding,
I feel Leo in every line of my fingerprint.
He is paint peeling on pubs in the Laines.
He is waves and pebbles,
I see his name written

in the cement of pavements.
He is no longer the pain
of rope burn, the dulled days.
This room is empty without him.
He passed like a train
that slows at a station
but then carries on,
taking no passengers, just leaving
expectant eyes. But he is safe.

And then I go home. E3.To Lockhart street. It seems miles away
from all the other streets I've ever lived on but it is my own. I
made it what it is with the girls who buy me pints before I'm
paid, who wipe tears away with loo roll, who sleep in my bed
when I don't want to wake up alone, who helped me find home.
Where photos of them hang behind magnets on the fridge. Where
wine bottles always need recycling. Where Sunday night dinners
roll into kitchen table confessionals. Where I sleep better than
anywhere I've ever been. All my dreams live in this unassuming
terrace. And they are closer to my hands now from where they
once were. A short walk from the canal and our favourite pub.
Where we struggle to make rent each month but there's so much
love trodden into the green carpet.

Sometimes I sit on buses with no destination in mind, looking
into flats and on the streets, people speaking to one another. I find
comfort in the stories of strangers, imagining how they've lived,
all they've faced. In Streatham the other day, I watched an old
woman stood in the snow. Brim of her hat pulled low, smoke from
her cigarillo rising above her head and curling up the steamed-up
shop-front of the Polish supermarket. She'd seen stuff, I reckon.
All laughter lines and memories rustling under her trench coat. Or
pensioner Lil...

I found her in the shallow end of Mile End leisure centre pool.
I'd been going there to keep my mind quiet. Pushing water with
breaststroke that mum had taught me. Lil remarked on my bikini.
Electric blue. Said it was nice to see young girls down the pool,
reminded her of her youth.
I've got six sons. Three were mine, three my husband's, but I always
felt like their mother. Love is love. And you have to approach life with
an open heart. I don't see them much anymore. Life gets in the way.
But I'm a woman of simple pleasures. Always down here on a Monday.
Important to keep active.

She waded away from me. Turned round.
Chin up girl. It could be worse.

She motioned for a lifeguard to help her out of the pool.
Nice strong arms, she said. Winked at me and flashed a gold tooth.

There's a house by Devons road where an old man hangs out of his skylights and waves at trains. I see him almost every day. He's always smiling.

This is nowhere near over yet. You just carry on, don't you? What other option do you have? And hope that one day, you'll find home. Or the closest thing to home you'll ever know. But that's just fine.

Meg comes in. She sits at the bar. Me on the other side polishing glasses. She's pressing her fingers hard against her empty wine glass.

Top up? I ask.
How are you? She says.
Better, I say.
I've been thinking, and I've been writing a bit lately. Want to hear some?

She fills her glass to the brim and nods for me to do the same.

Okay.

ACKNOWLEDGEMENTS

Thank you to my Dad for endless dinners and pints and advice and love, and to Hal for the relentless piss taking. Thank you Mum, we miss you everyday. Thank you to the Julies for being my sisters. Thank you to all my friends and family and to Emma . Thank you to the wonderful people I've met whilst being a writer, to the VC who have been there from the start and to Polarbear who helped me find my voice and listened to an early draft of this. Thank you to Liz and Stef who believed in my story and made it happen, to Charlie for always being by my side and making beautiful work, to all the audiences we've shown it to in development and in full, to the Roundhouse producers for their guidance and trust.

And Jordan, I am a better person because I know you.

Lightning Source UK Ltd.
Milton Keynes UK
UKOW06f0421260917
309835UK00009BA/158/P